Also available in this series from Quadrille:

the little book of
# MIND -FUL- NESS

the little book of
# QUIET

the little book of
# FRIENDSHIP

the little book of
# LOVE

the little book of
# CONFIDENCE

# MINDFUL TRAVEL

Tiddy Rowan

quadrille

*"If we wait for the moment when everything, absolutely everything is ready, we shall never begin."*

IVAN TURGENEV

So often we travel focused on our destination – whether it's a journey by car, train, plane, or walking. But once the destination is established, it's important to be aware of the process. Each step or part of the journey is what's happening in the present moment – the destination is still in the future.

*"We want to make good time, but for us now, this is measured with the emphasis on 'good' rather than on 'time'..."*

ROBERT M PIRSIG
*Zen and the Art of Motorcycle Maintenance:
An Inquiry into Values*

Physical travel can be seen as an analogy for the constant treks our minds make – the destination of the travel journey becomes the goal of our mental ones. We plan our day, the week, the weekend, next month, next year, five year plans when we retire. We create mind destinations, but they are not always mindful ones. A mindful destination is a goal we make with the understanding that it is in the getting there, every step along the way, that is important. Successful goals are a balance between initiative, discipline, and knowing when to let things proceed on their own.

**Ideally there is no such thing as a boring journey. Even the perceived tedium of the commuter's journey can be re-examined.**

There are a number of ways to spend the time. As soon as the commuter detaches from the immediate past (departure) and future (arrival), they are free to explore any one of an abundance of ideas, thoughts, or issues. Instead of resorting to a jumble of home- or work-related thoughts, some order can be introduced. A topic can be selected from the mental filing cabinet and explored methodically – but not randomly, mindfully.

Commuting to work is a good opportunity to practise gentle breathing exercises. They will keep you anchored in the present moment, clear your head, get oxygen to your brain, and relax you ready for the day's work.

This is also good practice when the journey is to an interview or presentation. Time spent this way – or at least part of it – is more productive than furiously cramming information into an already overloaded mind.

The same is true of the journey home. It is a chance to create space between work and home life and not take a jumble of unresolved problems through the front door. They can wait to be addressed, fresh, on the way to work tomorrow.

### The 'instant tranquillizer'

The 'Sigh Breath' is a simple breathing method for releasing tension. It can be an excellent way of managing the symptoms of anxiety or panic, staying calm before take off, or any other travel situation where we need to maintain, or regain, our equilibrium.

1. Inhale a moderate (rather than deep) breath through the nose.

2. Hold the breath for just a beat.

3. Allow the air to exhale very slowly through the nose or mouth – whichever comes more naturally.

4. Repeat, slowly, twice more.

5. Consciously allow the breaths to take their own natural rhythm until they become slower and shallower.

## Travel tips

To prevent muscle cramp on a long journey in a crowded train or plane, practise isometric exercises. It is a method of exercising using your own body weight as resistance (without an outward show of physical movement).

You can achieve a surprisingly good workout with seated isometric exercises, which can also significantly lower your blood pressure (or prevent it rising in a crowded or stressed environment).

But as with all exercise, it is advisable to check with your doctor first.

Being aware of fellow travellers is worthy of mindful attention. Everyone has their own story, their own journey and their own preoccupations. Allow them space – and courtesy.

*"To be mindful is to be truly alive, present and at one with those around you and with what you are doing."*

THICH NHAT HANH

*"Travel brings power and love back into your life."*

RUMI

### Travel tip

The golden rules for baggage:

- The rule of thumb is width + length + height = 114cm (45in).

- The optimum size bag or case to travel with is 35.6 x 28 x 50.8cm (14 x 11 x 20in).

- Choose a bag with square ends (rather than rounded or oval shaped) as it doesn't waste 'empty' corners.

- A bag this size fits in the majority of airline overhead lockers and conforms to carry-on luggage rules.

- With careful thought, you can pack into a bag this size enough luggage for a few days or a week or more, depending on the type of journey.

### Backpack or wheels?

A well-crafted backpack is the best way to carry your own luggage, especially if your travelling involves less beaten tracks. There are many to choose from – designed for weight distribution, balance, and optimum packing space. The beauty of this is that it leaves your hands free.

With a wheelie bag the weight of the inbuilt wheels adds to your luggage allowance; wheels do not cope well with cobbles, uneven terrains, or steps, so there will still be some carrying to do. But it is the next best option for one-stop city destinations.

*"He who would travel happily must travel light."*

ANTOINE DE SAINT-EXUPÉRY

We all carry around so much mental baggage – from essential data to stored memories and anticipated hopes and objectives. It's hardly surprising that there is so much stress in our frantic to-ing and fro-hing. A journey – any journey – offers a good opportunity to clear the mind. Pack an imaginary case and put in it only the essential data, memories, and immediate goals that you can reasonably cope with. Lighten the load on a daily basis. Think of the mind as having hand baggage and stowed baggage. On an everyday basis carry only what you need. The rest can be accessed when needed.

"*Let your boat of life be light, packed with only what you need – a homely home and simple pleasures, one or two friends, worth the name, someone to love and someone to love you, a cat, a dog, and a pipe or two, enough to eat and enough to wear, and a little more than enough to drink; for thirst is a dangerous thing.*"

JEROME K. JEROME
*Three Men in a Boat*

### Travel tip

When idling in a café abroad, and keen not to be disturbed but left to people-watch in peace, carry a folded newspaper in the language of the country you're in. Of course, you might be asked directions by an unsuspecting compatriot, but it will cut down on the unwanted attention from tourist pests offering you tour guides/gondola rides/hashish/their sister (depending on your location and gender). At least you won't look like a sitting duck. And you can always put your newspaper of choice within the decoy for a leisurely read.

*"There are no foreign lands.*
*It is the traveller only who is foreign."*

ROBERT LOUIS STEVENSON
*The Silverado Squatters*

Somewhere along the road, there comes the realization of return. Returning is significant since it highlights where our vital centre lies; it defines our roots, or lack of them. In making our way home, we are, in effect, aware of returning to our own centre. However rich or varied our explorations into new terrain, be it physically, creatively, or mentally, from time to time it is important to come back to our centre – to our own mothership and core.

*"No one realizes how beautiful it is to travel until he comes home and rests his head on his old, familiar pillow."*

**LIN YUTANG**
*The Importance of Living*

There are times when we want to travel back, to revisit places out of a sense of nostalgia, of longing for something already finished in the past. How often is that journey an unsatisfactory one? The hotel has been taken over by developers, the favourite bar is no longer there, the beach – once a secret haven – is now crowded. The treasured memory is eradicated. A reminder, perhaps, that we cannot relive our past but can, instead, focus on our present lives, enjoy new experiences and seek new horizons. Or return with an awareness that it will be as a new experience, not reliving an old one.

## Be adventurous!

Going to places that we have visited before, to places we already know, begs the question whether familiarity removes the appeal of travel itself – the fascination of the unknown.

At least once a year go somewhere you have never travelled to before, either abroad or in your home country.

If you can be truly at one with the journey, you become less self-conscious as a traveller and more in tune with the present moments of your life. Practising mindfulness is conducive to being *part* of the journey, rather than being *apart* from it. To be always thinking of where we have to 'be' next, or to be overly concerned about missing a travel connection is to negate living in the now. Even a delay can bring unexpected pleasures – a chance encounter, an enforced rest, or avoiding an unforeseen mishap – so having a travel plan is one thing, but being open to change is another.

The wrong train can sometimes take you to the right place.

Travelling encourages a sense of optimism. You cannot help but travel hopefully. Otherwise you wouldn't – or possibly shouldn't! – travel at all.

Even a basic knowledge of the historical, political, and sociological landscape of the area you're visiting gives a richer involvement and understanding of the place and the people when you arrive. Lying in a hammock on an idyllic beach be the chosen destination for your well-earned holiday, though an awareness of how local people may live with poverty will help remind us of our good fortune, despite any struggles, many of us live relatively rich lives.

Respecting religious and social traditions and customs leads to a quicker integration with the people of the country we are visiting. It is invaluable spending time researching and understanding these traditions and different ways of life as a matter of compassion and good manners.

This is true whether it is a business or pleasure visit.

*"If you reject the food, ignore the customs, fear the religion, and avoid the people, you might better stay home."*

JAMES A. MICHENER

*Good Advice*

When we are at home and using a shared language to communicate, we are less aware of our body language. Conversely, when we are in an environment where we don't know the language, we rely on other signals. The eyes convey warmth, hostility, or alarm. We can develop our skill in reading these signals as well as being mindful of our own physical cues. Being cold, hungry, or tired are states that simple sign language conveys. It is a stark reminder of our basic and universal human needs, which are understood throughout the world, and require no words.

> "*The place to improve the world is first in one's own heart and head and hands, and then work outward from there.*"

ROBERT M. PIRSIG
*Zen and the Art of Motorcycle Maintenance:*
*An Inquiry into Values*

### Take a digital holiday

Instead of time spent on gadget screens and mobile phones, spend the time talking to people on your journey. Being more in the present space – and less in the one you have temporarily left behind – rewards you with an increased awareness of the world, of fresh stimuli, different and unexpected forms of entertainment, new friendships and new horizons.

## Photography and travel

The efficiency of cameras combined with the urge to take pictures home to talk about, renders the actual moment less imperative. Don't fall into the habit of always experiencing the moment through the lens of a camera. It's interesting to take (selective) pictures to have reminders of special occasions or people, but it is not a substitute for being fully present in that moment or retaining the image or experience in the mind's eye. Capturing a moment in order to look at it in the future is to miss experiencing the moment in the present.

### Don't over plan

Whilst it may be efficient to have a tight schedule, over zealous planning is to always be thinking about the future and missing the actual moment. Surely part of the joy of travelling is to be less bound by the calendar, less stressed about dates and times, and allowing the mind to slow down and adapt to a more carefree schedule in contrast to the demanding work environment that we seek to escape.

*"The best of travel seems to exist outside of time, as though the years of travel are not deducted from your life."*

PAUL THEROUX
*Ghost Train to the Eastern Star*

## Food... for thought

Be selective in literary companions: something to absorb, something to instruct, something to amuse.

A well-chosen paperback to read on your journey could start an exchange. Leave it somewhere for another reader to find or give it to a fellow traveller, then have fun selecting the next. For all other books and journals on the move, economy of space might necessitate an e-reader or e-book. Function over form, but with the pleasure of having at least one physical book to turn to.

### Food... for travel

When travelling our digestive system becomes disorientated. We tend to eat all the wrong things out of boredom or habit. Peanuts, crisps, biscuits, pre-packed sandwiches, fizzy drinks, alcohol... all these play havoc with our digestive systems. We rely on food that is often the only thing to hand – from roadside garages, station newsagents, fast food outlets, or in-flight food.

What the body needs is simple fuel and hydration: high protein food, healthy snacks, and water. Avoid heavy meals the day before travelling. The digesting clock is some hours behind the travelling clock and needs 'packing' consideration too.

"*I have found out that there ain't no surer way to find out whether you like people or hate them than to travel with them.*"

MARK TWAIN
*Tom Sawyer Abroad*

## To travel alone or with company?

A short break or a holiday is happily shared with a lover or a friend, but unless you're certain of the relationship, travelling of a more inquiring kind is best done alone. A chance to think, to absorb, to be spontaneous without the commentary, interruptions, or alternative plans of other people. Whatever the personal preference, everyone should experience the solitude, the random social encounters, the personal highs of a journey alone at some point. Even the most gregarious of people benefit from time out.

*"When there is no one to remind you what society's rules are, and there is nothing to keep you linked to that society, you had better be prepared for some startling changes."*

ROBYN DAVIDSON
*Tracks*

John Tagholm celebrated his fiftieth birthday by walking the footpaths across France on his own. Writing in his book *Elsewhere*, John observed the path on which he walked '... will be here long after I have gone, a tunnel through time, linking the past and the future, with the here and the now.'

A good thought to meditate on as a mindful walking exercise.

Walking has a natural pace to it – we find it instinctively, as we do with the rhythm of our breath, and we walk according to the pace we feel is right. The motion invigorates us, prevents restlessness, keeps us occupied, and allows for a mental detox. At first we might walk at a fast pace, furious about something, a feeling of being coiled up with anger, disappointment, worry, or resentment. But after walking a while, our pace slackens and without consciously realizing it, our mental pace imperceptibly slackens too.

Robert Macfarlane reflects in his book
*The Old Ways: A Journey on Foot*
on the Edwardian poet-naturalist
Edward Thomas. 'To Thomas,'
Macfarlane observes, 'paths connected
real places but they also led outwards
to metaphysics, backwards to history
and inwards to the self.'

'The mind', to Edward Thomas, 'was
a landscape of a kind and walking a
means of crossing it.'

*"Wandering re-establishes the original harmony which once existed between man and the universe."*

ANATOLE FRANCE

*"To practice walking meditation is to practice living in mindfulness. Mindfulness and enlightenment are one. Enlightenment leads to mindfulness and mindfulness leads to enlightenment."*

THICH NHAT HANH

Taking on some form of exercise, health training, or a spiritual quest all require commitment and daily discipline. But sometimes the willpower is lacking or the challenge seems too demanding and we experience failure or a sense of futility. By viewing the undertaking as a journey we can be reassured that the destination can not be reached in one leap. It takes time to climb a mountain: we stumble on loose rocks and have to pick ourselves up and continue. We are rewarded the next day with improved resolve, a refreshed outlook or view, and the incentive to keep going.

*"So, if you cannot understand that there is something in man which responds to the challenge of this mountain and goes out to meet it, that the struggle is the struggle of life itself upward and forever upward, then you won't see why we go."*

GEORGE LEIGH MALLORY

Sailing is for many people a meaningful analogy for the itinerary of our lives. Even for non-sailors the notions of direction, focus, planning, learning to read weather patterns, taking storms in our strides, and dealing with being blown off course are conditions we can relate to, both in physical experience as well as in our minds. Relating the more difficult experiences in life to the analogies of sailing and the weather helps us to understand that storms pass and they are best dealt with on a practical level rather than an emotional one.

*"A ship in harbour is safe,*
*but that is not what ships are built for."*

JOHN A. SHEDD
*Salt from My Attic*

How often do we travel to 'get away', referring to the usual circumstances of our home-/work-life patterns? More often what we mean is that we want to 'get away' from our selves.

Travel can bring about certain changes, but there can be a sense of disappointment when we are still bothered by difficult feelings we had before we left home. The antidote is to spend time in mindful contemplation in order to stay in front of the continued present moments of our lives. Wherever we are.

*"I pack my trunk, embrace my friends, embark on the sea and at last wake up in Naples, and there beside me is the stern fact, the sad self, unrelenting, identical, that I fled from."*

RALPH WALDO EMERSON

### Greetings

The importance of that first impression we make on the people we meet along the way, or the people we travel to meet at our destination, are embodied in our greeting. Different cultures, different styles of greeting all contain a unique etiquette. Despite possible weariness of the journey behind us, it's important to focus on the present moment, not recent past, in order to always greet others with a cheerful disposition.

*"Always greet life with a smile."*

CHINESE BUDDHIST PROVERB

## Greeting customs

**France:** Even French people are unsure which cheek to present, or how many kisses to give. Offering the right cheek to start with seems the general rule. How many kisses depends on familiarity, friendship, or family – at least two kisses, a third on better acquaintance, and expect anything up to five. Children and adults alike shake hands and kiss each other on meeting and when they say goodbye.

**Europe:** Two cheek kisses, or a handshake if you're meeting for the first time.

**UK:** A handshake is the norm, though cheek-kissing is becoming more prevalent.

**USA:** Handshakes are the norm; European-style kisses, especially between women.

**Thailand:** Put your hands together in a prayer pose and lower your head in a bow so that your forehead touches your fingertips.

**China:** The traditional greeting involves folding one hand over the other and shaking them together and offering a cupped-hand bow. In formal situations, lowering your head shows respect. Otherwise handshakes are widely accepted.

**India:** When conducting business or around Westerners a handshake is commonplace. A typical greeting in a relaxed or local situation is to put your palms together in the prayer pose, incline your head and say 'Namaste'.

On the returning part of the journey, it is important to strengthen our sense of awareness. We travel with the vague notion that everything will stay the same whilst we're away and we will slip back into old patterns. But an increased awareness at the point of homecoming allows for a merging of our new experiences with perceived differences at our home hub. If we mistake transience for permanence, then we are bound to encounter problems. By remembering that we are all part of ever-changing and ever-evolving circumstances, then our continued journey back home will be infused with lightness and clarity.

*"Wherever you go,*
*go with all your heart."*

CONFUCIUS

The flow of rivers, the tides, and the vastness of the oceans can be compared to our own passage through life. A certain understanding of, and need for, navigation is an imperative tool on our voyage; just as an ability to float with the waves is also vital.

It is not just the comparison that is worth reflecting on, but also the fact that we are part of the rivers and oceans and that the consequences of our actions affect the very water that is our basic constituent ingredient. (The body's composition is 60% water.)

*"Our deeds still travel with us from afar, and what we have been makes us what we are."*

GEORGE ELIOT (MARY ANN CROSS)
*Middlemarch*

We take maps for granted. From the earliest map making – the mappa mundi drawn in c.1285 is the largest known medieval map in the world – we have now come to rely on satellite navigation to easily lead us from one place to another.

Contemplating the night sky reminds us of the importance of stars in guiding mariners.

It's not too whimsical, perhaps, to compare maps and stars to the course of our spiritual journey through life. Philosophers, teachers, educators, mentors, and books all play a part in our mental voyage.

### Mapping the mind

Take a large sheet of plain paper and 'map' your mind to see what spontaneously evolves.

Draw a large circle and identify yourself within it.

Fill in dots or spokes radiating from the centre of the circle and see what you attribute to these fixed or guiding dots and goals – like a road map.

However you doodle or draw this image it will create a reflection of how you view your life. Not unlike creating a personal mandala, it can become something to contemplate and add to as a way of objectively evaluating where you are in life.

*"Perhaps, then, this was what travelling was, an exploration of the deserts of my mind rather than of those surrounding me?"*

CLAUDE LÉVI-STRAUSS
*Tristes Tropiques*

There are many pathways open to those who seek to explore routes into the subconscious, whether on a spiritual journey or simply to better understand the terrain that is the mind, the personality – the self. We don't have to go on a physical journey to experience quests of this type.

Understanding the characteristics of boundaries is to understand their limitations. Constraints are not necessarily negative restrictions – they define a given situation. Without knowing where the edge is, it's easy to go over it – and fall. Everything has a limit; the mindful person tries to identify where that limit is, then holds back to conserve energy. This is relevant in business matters, in personal relationships, in understanding what other peoples' limitations might be; it is relevant in physical exercise, and in undertaking a trek or a journey.

*"A journey of a thousand miles starts with a single step."*

LAO TZU

We tend to regard certain objects
or matters as fixtures in our lives.
But like the flow of a river altering due
to a fallen boulder, we also need to
flow around people or circumstances
that appear or change unexpectedly.
Conversely we can consciously
shift matters, or our perceptions, to
alter the flow of life and of energy.
Practising mindfulness breathing
exercises enhances our awareness
of this constant flow of energy that
is not only within us, but to which we
are connected.

*"Whither will my path yet lead me?
This path is stupid, it goes in spirals,
perhaps in circles, but whichever way
it goes, I will follow it."*

HERMANN HESSE
*Siddhartha*

## How does the view of the visitor differ from that of a resident?

Parisians walk past the Eiffel Tower every day on their way to work whilst others fly across the world to experience the view.

A way of getting a telescopic glimpse of this paradox is to choose a spot in your home town or country and, as a mindful exercise, sit quietly and observe and listen. Really connect with the space as though you are experiencing it for the first time. Go a step further and imagine you are now observing it all through the eyes of a visitor from another country. It reinforces the importance of looking at things – both physical and non-physical – with fresh eyes.

*"Weary with toil, I haste me to my bed,*
*The dear repose for limbs with travel tired;*
*But then begins a journey in my head*
*To work my mind, when body's work's*
*expired."*

WILLIAM SHAKESPEARE

When we travel as tourists our viewpoints are often directed by guidebooks. This encourages a trip full of sightseeing and may mean missing out on our own discoveries.

Be flexible in over-planning your itinerary, make sure that you can still be spontaneous. There can be as much pleasure in coming across hidden gems and places you find on your own, as following the well-beaten track to – and all too often crowded – famous sights.

*"Not till we are lost...,*
*do we begin to find ourselves."*

HENRY DAVID THOREAU

Visiting an art gallery allows you to mindfully travel whilst standing still. By viewing a particular landscape you can travel in your imagination, drawn in by the accomplishment of the artist who has stood in the same spot, sharing their observation through their art. You can be truly transported to another place and time.

Literature depicts a sense of place. Each of us has our favourite places where writers have taken us along with them.

Consider F. Scott Fitzgerald, Alain-Fournier, Tom Robbins, Ivan Turgenev, Arthur C. Clarke, Karen Blixen, Robyn Davidson, William Dalrymple, Colin Thubron, Jan Morris, Eric Newby, Patrick Leigh Fermor, John Steinbeck, Bill Bryson, Jack Kerouac, Laurie Lee, Julian Barnes, Jonathan Raban, Graham Greene, Paul Theroux, Bruce Chatwin, Redmond O'Hanlon, Mark Twain, to mention a few.

Imagine all the travelling we can do simply by choosing the right books to transport us.

*"We travel not to escape life,
but so that life does not escape us."*

ANONYMOUS

*"Our battered suitcases were piled on the sidewalk again; we had longer ways to go. But no matter, the road is life."*

JACK KEROUAC
*On the Road*

Why is there such a constant travel bug? What generates this nomadic-like desire to travel?

We visit capital cities, search out lakes and mountaintops, sail the seas, and yet we rarely question 'Why?'

Our need to travel is as primordial as our need to sleep, to eat, to procreate. Our hunter-gatherer ancestors were nomads and many of us are becoming so again with the ease of foreign travel, long-distance commuting, digital nomadism, and a declining sense of national roots in any one place.

*"Travel, which was once either a necessity or an adventure, has become very largely a commodity, and from all sides we are persuaded into thinking that it is a social requirement, too."*

JAN MORRIS
*'It's O.K. to Stay at Home', New York Times, 30 August 1985*

Around 1660, the Grand Tour was conceived as a 'gap year', or essential rite of passage undertaken by members of English high society. They followed each other along a route through France to Paris then across the Alps to Switzerland, and on to Turin, Florence, Pisa, Bologna, Venice, the centrepiece of the Tour, and on to Rome. Some grand tourists travelled on to Greece, before heading home to England, stopping off in Austria, Germany, and the Netherlands on the way. The Tour, sometimes lasting years, spawned the idea of travelling for pleasure, for leisure, for curiosity – or to acquire skills and knowledge in classical studies.

*"Nothing can be compared to the new life that the discovery of another country provides for a thoughtful person. Although I am still the same I believe to have changed to the bones."*

JOHANN WOLFGANG VON GOETHE
*Italian Journey*

Cultural tourism is one of the largest and fastest-growing global tourism markets. Culture and creative industries are increasingly being used to promote destinations and enhance their competitiveness and attractiveness.

Many communities are now actively developing their cultural assets as a means of creating advantages in a competitive tourist market, and to create local distinctiveness in the face of globalization.

*"In an underdeveloped country don't drink the water. In a developed country don't breathe the air."*

JONATHAN RABAN

*"A journey is like marriage.
The certain way to be wrong
is to think you control it."*

JOHN STEINBECK
*Travels with Charley : In Search of America*

"*And if travel is like love, it is, in the end, mostly because it's a heightened state of awareness, in which we are mindful, receptive, undimmed by familiarity and ready to be transformed. That is why the best trips, like the best love affairs, never really end.*"

PICO IYER
*Why We Travel*

One of the many advantages of travel is that in old(er) age our travel experiences can be revisited. In fact it's amazing how, with mindful attention, we can re-trace so many of our earlier travels in the relative comfort of our homes. And adventures can be enjoyed repeatedly, like watching a favourite movie – but with all the tension removed since, we know they end well because we survived any jeopardy we might have experienced at the time.

**Talking to Florence, aged five, and listening to her notion of what is a journey...**

*"A journey is... you can go to different places and you can go far away on a journey. You can't walk it's too far, otherwise your legs will be hurting, but you always need a car or a truck. If you want to go far away you need a train, or a boat, or a plane, ... or a helicopter or... submarine or a scooter... or a trampoline so you can go really high like a space rocket ... OR... a magic carpet. But... you have to find a magic carpet – you can't buy one."*

*"It is good to have an end
to journey toward; but it is the
journey that matters, in the end."*

URSULA K. LE GUIN
*The Left Hand of Darkness*

Travelling – is to be in transit and on the road – which is the opposite of being stationery. Being in one place for too long can lead to stagnation and introspection, hence the importance of travel or change of scenery to refresh a point of view.

John Locke in his *Essay Concerning Human Understanding* suggests that knowledge is not innate, that it has to come from outside stimuli. In theory, a person could consume all the stimuli from their immediate environment and would then need to travel in order to gain further understanding and knowledge of the world.

*"Twenty years from now you will be more disappointed by the things you didn't do than the ones you did do. So throw off the bowlines. Sail away from the safe harbour. Catch the trade winds in your sails.*

*Explore. Dream. Discover."*

H. JACKSON BROWN, JNR
*P.S. I Love You: When Mom Wrote,
She Always Saved the Best for Last*

*"I dreamed a thousand new paths.
I woke and walked my old one."*

ANCIENT CHINESE PROVERB

We journey from day to night every 24 hours, yet we tend to leave to chance our quality of our sleep and whether we experience good dreams or bad ones.

If your sleep is erratic, keep a journal to help identify what might have contributed to either a good or a bad night and to see where to make changes.

If we were setting off on an eight-hour journey, we'd probably prepare for it in various ways. Perhaps we should apply the same mindfulness to the journey into night and create optimum 'travel' conditions.

*"The use of travelling is to regulate imagination by reality, and instead of thinking how things may be, to see them as they are."*

SAMUEL JOHNSON
*Letter to Hester Thrale*

*"All of the sights of the hill and the plain*
*Fly as thick as driving rain;*
*And ever again, in the wink of an eye,*
*Painted stations whistle by."*

ROBERT LOUIS STEVENSON
*From a Railway Carriage*

Most people have experienced sitting in the window seat of a train and have watched the landscape race past them.

There is, in that activity, the sense of truly capturing the future, the present, and the past. One moment the view ahead of us is somehow in the future, then it is in front of us, representing the fleeting present before it disappears behind us and into the past. Recent studies by neuroscientists suggest that 'now' lasts a couple of seconds. About the same time as the captured view from the train window.

Marc Wittmann at the Institute for Frontier Areas in Psychology and Mental Health in Freiburg, Germany, conducted a study of meditators and non-meditators. The meditators scored higher in tests of attention and memory capacity. 'If you are aware of what is happening around you, you not only experience more in the present moment you also have more memory content. Meditators perceive time to pass more slowly than non-meditators, both in the present and retrospectively,' he says.

This suggests that with some mindful attention we are all capable of developing fuller awareness of the present moment.

*"Travel makes one modest.
You see what a tiny place
you occupy in the world."*

GUSTAVE FLAUBERT
*Flaubert in Egypt: A Sensibility on Tour*

When we're travelling we tend to immerse ourselves in the here and now – revelling in our different circumstances and surroundings, thinking about the simpler things such as where to eat, where to watch the sunset, studying a map – instead of routinely being preoccupied by persistent concerns of work, bills, duties. The emphasis of a holiday is often concentrated on the body, but it is just as vital to loosen the ties of the mind and let it roam free for a while. Let the mind have some fun, in the same way that a child enjoys to play – free from fret.

*"But that's the glory of foreign travel, as far as I am concerned. I don't want to know what people are talking about."*

BILL BRYSON
*Neither Here nor There: Travels in Europe*

Many an armchair traveller has journeyed the world vicariously through the power of writing, their imagination activated and stirred through an author's adventures. The eccentric and aristocratic protagonist, Duc des Esseintes observed in the novel 'Against Nature' by Joris-Karl Huysmans:

*"Travel, indeed, struck him as being a waste of time, since he believed that... anyone can go on long voyages of exploration... if the need arises, by dipping into some book describing travels in distant lands."*

*"He didn't really like travel, of course. He liked the idea of travel, and the memory of travel, but not travel itself."*

JULIAN BARNES
*Flaubert's Parrot*

Knowing our motive for travel means that we can explore aspects of what this means to us along the way rather than expecting to find what we're looking for on arriving at a destination.

Whatever our purpose for travel (to enhance our confidence, to make new friends, to question or determine our beliefs, to seek happiness), it pays well to be mindful of the objective thus allowing the broadest opportunity for exploration of ourselves amongst the sights we see and the people we meet.

## Walking meditation

Japanese Zen gardens, as well as labyrinths, are conducive to walking meditation – effective tools for keeping the mind focused on the footsteps, the path, and the present moment, keeping anxious thoughts and internal chatter at bay, and giving the mind a chance to unwind and sift through data subconsciously – and effectively.

Walking meditation is very simple. Aim your gaze a few steps ahead, and free your mind of all thoughts and emotions, directing your awareness towards each foot as you place it on the ground. Focus on your footsteps, and when your mind wanders from this focus, bring it back to your feet.

" *It is a pity indeed to travel and not get this essential sense of landscape values. You do not need a sixth sense for it. It is there if you just close your eyes and breathe softly through your nose; you will hear the whispered message, for all landscapes ask the same question in the same whisper. 'I am watching you – are you watching yourself in me?' Most travellers hurry too much... the great thing is to try and travel with the eyes of the spirit wide open, and not too much factual information. To tune in, without reverence, idly – but with real inward attention.* "

**LAWRENCE DURRELL**
*Spirit of Place: Letters and Essays on Travel*

*"The traveller sees what he sees. The tourist sees what he has come to see."*

G.K. CHESTERTON

**Mindful packing**

Really think ahead to what the purpose of your trip is and visualize what you will want, or need to be wearing. If you're not sure, then try combinations on before you pack, rather than taking something that 'might' work. Ideally everything should go with everything, giving maximum options.

Don't forget to pack something that you like chilling in. It's surprising how much time can be spent being 'at home' staying with people, in a hotel or apartment, beach hut etc.

There is a packing adage, which is good advice for anyone:

*"When preparing to travel, lay out all your clothes and all your money. Then take half the clothes and twice the money."*

SUSAN HELLER ANDERSON

*Getting the Show on the Road, The New York Times*

*(29 March 1987)* .

When planning a journey, anxieties often arise over the issue of packing. What to take? Which bag? Carry-on or hold? Further anxieties can develop over locating passports, security of the house whilst away, where to leave the cat, getting everything in order, right up until the moment of boarding the plane or train, or setting off in the car.

Once the journey or holiday is decided upon – tickets are bought, time out is allotted – then savour the preparation. There is much pleasure to be had in the anticipation of the journey. Stay mindful not to let that pleasure be buried in a stressful departure.

*"Here today, up and off to somewhere else tomorrow! Travel, change, interest, excitement! The whole world before you, and a horizon that's always changing!"*

KENNETH GRAHAME
*The Wind in the Willows*

Travel and tourism represents approximately 9.5% of total global Gross Domestic Product (GDP). The global travel and tourism industry creates approximately 10% of the world's employment (direct and indirect).

At least 25 million people spread over 52 countries are displaced by violence, persecution, and disasters. Tourism in places affected is often a key source of finance, and a decline in economy adds to the anguish and downturn of their adversity. So tourist money, spent thoughtfully can help these countries.

Paradoxically, the downside of mass tourism is the impact it can have on local environments.

The average person in the UK uses approximately 150 litres (264 pints) of water a day – three times that of a local villager, in Asia. A European consumes fourteen times the energy of someone living in India.

The Western world (with 17% of the world's population) currently consumes 52% of total global energy.

We need to travel more mindfully in the way we use (or misuse) available water and energy.

*sustainabletourism.net*

## Recycling abroad

Many people adopt green habits at home, through conscientious good habits, conforming to guidelines, or for fear of facing penalties for mixing up their recycling – but it is important to practise environmentally sound habits whilst also on holiday.

The message is: take your (good) green habits away with you when you travel.

## What is sustainable tourism?

" *Sustainable tourism is tourism committed to generating a low impact on the surrounding environment and community by acting responsibly while generating income and employment for the local economy and aiding social cohesion.* "

To some good effect, The World Heritage Committee launched the World Heritage Sustainable Tourism Programme in 2001. The programme focuses on maintaining a balance between sustainable tourism and conservation.

We need to consider how much to travel in environmentally sensitive areas. The Antarctic Treaty places strict limits on tourism to prevent damage to the pristine environment. Bhutan has for years protected its natural environment from the damage witnessed in neighbouring countries by rationing tourism, limiting visas, and keeping their prices high. Keep sustainability in mind when planning your trips.

*whytravel.org*

Managing tourism is about refocusing and adapting. A balance must be found between limits and usage so that continuous adapting, monitoring, and planning ensure that tourism can be well-handled. This requires thinking long-term and realizing that change is often cumulative, gradual, and irreversible. Economic, social, and environmental aspects of sustainable development must include the interests of all parties – including indigenous people, local communities, visitors, industry, and government.

Be a conscientious tourist

**Avoid excessive waste and the use of plastic bottles.** In many countries there is no means of disposing of them, thereby creating plastic mountains due to tourism.

**Reduce energy consumption.** Unplug your mobile phone charger once it's charged. Turn off lights. Conserve water. Take shorter showers. The average hotel guest uses over 300 litres (528 pints) of water per night.

**Use cloth or reusable bags for shopping instead of plastic bags.**

**Support responsible tourism organizations.**

## More tips for the mindful tourist

**Ask permission before taking photographs.** If someone says no, respect their wishes.

**Respect cultural differences.** People in different places do things differently. Don't try to change them, learn from them, and enjoy them.

**Do not purchase or eat endangered species.**

**Support the local economy.** Buy locally made art and crafts, eat at local restaurants, enjoy the local culture.

**Offset your flight.** Neutralize carbon emissions by offsetting your flight.

**Use public transportation.** Whenever and wherever possible, use the train, bus, cycle, or walk.

**Maintaining conscientious tourism
and travel:**

If you're not part of the solution,
you're part of the problem.

There is a real danger that tourism can displace local residents through the demand for accommodation hiking property prices, usually purchased by large multinational hotels.

Joan Oliveras, President of Amicas de Las Rambla in Barcelona, Spain, warns 'Tourists visit a city because it is alive. When a zone becomes a platform for tourism and nothing else, the interest in the place dies.'

Support smaller hotels and local guest houses.

However you're travelling – in a group, with a partner, friend, or alone – budget travel can be much more rewarding and not just for saving money. Public transport, eating in non-tourist restaurants/cafés/bars, and staying in family run guest houses and hotels will give you a far better insight into local customs and culture than staying in five-star 'international' hotels and travelling around in first class luxury. It also spreads visitors out, away from the clusters of mass tourism.

*"It can hardly be a coincidence that no language on earth has ever produced the expression, 'As pretty as an airport'."*

DOUGLAS ADAMS
*The Long Dark Tea-Time of the Soul*

There is a tendency to categorize other people by nationality. As though we're no longer individuals but only a nationality with a collective personality and behaviour. Does this categorizing create an unnecessary barrier between people of different nationalities, as though we are all inherently different as human beings?

Through exercises to strengthen our mindfulness, understanding, and sense of compassion, we can be more aware of our own development and place in humanity.

*"Travel is fatal to prejudice, bigotry and narrow-mindedness, and many of our people need it sorely on those accounts. Broad, wholesome, charitable views of men and things cannot be acquired by vegetating in one little corner of the earth all one's lifetime."*

MARK TWAIN
*Innocents Abroad*

Travelling can act as a reminder that other people have their own moral and social structures – developed over time and generations – that our way is not the only way, or even that our basic needs, wants, and compassion to others are essentially shared and the same. Aren't we all striving for the same things ultimately?

Keeping a common goal in mind might make us more mindful of how we journey together towards that shared, more enlightened destination.

*"Travel and change of place impart new vigour to the mind."*

SENECA

**The basic points of mindfulness:**

1. Being still.

2. Being aware.

3. Being non-judgemental towards yourself and others.

4. Bask in the present. Make the present last longer than a fleeting moment in time. Make time a continuing present moment.

Cherish your feet. How many steps have they taken for you on your journey through life? How many miles a year do they carry us around?

Away from home we tend to put more strain on our feet as we explore cities, hike mountains, carry luggage around. Good walking shoes, good socks, inner soles, foot massage, foot soaks are all good investments of time and money.

Walk around barefoot in your house when you can – in the morning and when you come in from a day's work. It keeps us literally grounded, we are more aware of the work our feet do for us... .

Wherever you're going – and particularly if you're going a long distance and can choose the time of year – make sure you plan the optimum season so as to avoid rainy seasons, hurricane seasons, or temperatures that soar uncomfortably high. There will be enough range in the weather without having to wade straight into a monsoon or a capital city in sweltering heat.

## Dehydration

If the quality of tap water is uncertain and there is no available bottled water or means to boil it, cola is an effective alternative. Drunk flat and without ice it can help deal with stomach upsets. Boiled, then simmered with fresh ginger provides a good remedy for a cold or sore throat.

Dehydration can lead to headaches, dizziness, fatigue, and more serious medical conditions. So it's important to keep hydrated. Sipping little and often is preferable to gulping volumes to try and compensate for a lack of fluids.

Avoid plastic water bottles. Take a flask, which you can constantly refill.

Keeping some form of travel journal or notebook will pay dividends when you get home and want to be reminded of some experiences, thoughts, ideas, sketches. We think we will remember every detail, but we don't. Having even the briefest of notes gives pleasure long after we've returned home.

Write letters to family and friends whilst you're away. Travelling allows more time for reflection and relaxation. Writing by hand brings out fresh thoughts and observations. You have the time to write at a different pace. It will also enrich the digital record of your holiday.

If you're musical and like playing an instrument, get yourself a harmonica. Even a cheap one takes up no room and is good for playing scales, improving your breathing, and you never know when you might find yourself at an impromptu celebration or birthday party.

Being able to play even rudimentary chess is a good travelling skill. It needs no common language other than that of mindful play (as do most board games and a lot of card games). Carry a pack of cards with you for spontaneous social encounters whilst travelling. A frisbee doesn't take up much room and – if you're planning on camping or backpacking with other people – it's a great form of exercise and interplay.

Practising mindfulness doesn't mean you have to sign up for courses. It can be accessed in an instant.

At the root of mindfulness is meditation and breathing. With attention to the breath going in and out you naturally deflect random thoughts and stay rooted in the present moment. If you practise breathing exercises you will find a calmness which provides the right state in which to meditate.

Everyone's mind wanders, but since there is no judgment you can return, without anxiety, to the breathing and the meditating. Keeping a sense of lightness and ease.

When you want to explore further, consider travelling to a place to learn more about the practice of mindfulness and the lifelong benefits you will derive.

Seek out retreats and places that provide sanctuary or a combination of classes and time to unwind, combining travel with a sense of mindfulness.

"*Slow down and taste and smell and hear, and let your senses come alive. If you want a royal road to mysticism, sit down quietly and listen to all the sounds around you.*"

ANTHONY DE MELLO
*Awareness*

### Taste

Give your taste buds a holiday too. Experiment with local food and flavours. Have papaya and lime for breakfast, an enchilada or fish kebab from a street stall for lunch. Try things you have never tasted before, especially whatever is fresh and available locally. New spices, herbs, edible flowers all enliven the palate and the moment, and enrich our understanding and connection to the local cuisine and the country's culture. After all, you have the time to slow down and savour the food, the company, and the surrounding landscape or activities.

## Sight

When travelling our eyes focus keenly on horizons near and far, giving the muscles of our eyes beneficial exercise.

Enjoy the change of light in different places, notice how shadows grow, how colours become saturated or bleached out in bright sunshine. Observe the way some colours appear differently abroad than they do at home. The contrast in colours in the Mediterranean and India to the northern hemisphere is striking. Colours are uplifting. We can enjoy them afresh in a new light, new landscapes, textiles, spices and vegetable markets, plants, and art.

## Touch

Feel the warmth of the sun on a rock, trail fingers through the sand, tread the seabed beneath bare feet, touch rough stone walls. Sense the tactility of different materials, a feather-light breeze or salt-whipped spray from the sea on your face... be aware of the many different surfaces your hands and feet touch.

**Smell**

Relish new scents from exotic flowers,
especially white ones which perfume
the evening air, the smell of sea and
sun on the skin, unfamiliar fresh
ground coffee, spicy cooking,
unusual scents, vegetation after
heavy rainfall, bonfires burning
with different local wood.

## Hearing

Bells, unfamiliar sirens, chatter, kitchen clatter, the cadence of voices speaking in a different language, different birdsong, animal noises, music – all add to our rounded experience of travel.

In fact, bells and sirens can be used as calls to mindfulness – to bring us back, consciously, into the moment, a prompt to drop the shoulders and take a few gentle breaths.

Source music local to the places you are visiting to add to your collection of world music. Record unusual sounds, dawn chorus, the laughter of children, or night waves breaking on a crunchy shore to use as an accompaniment to meditation.

The benefits of travelling light are many: less toll on the shoulders, knowing you have all your belongings with you, confident you can manage your luggage without help, making public transportation easier and more cost effective (no need for taxis), and saving money on expensive add-ons for in-hold luggage on budget airlines.

Anyone who has switched to travelling with less knows the feeling of lightness not only for the body but also for the mind, producing a sense of freedom.

Seasoned packers remain divided between the 'roll it' or the 'pack it flat' options.

Either way you have the option of using compression bags within the case which, when squeezed, extract air and hence reduce density. Useful for light jumpers, t-shirts, underwear and fleeces.

**The choice of fabric when travelling is important.**

Denim, heavy drill cotton, and some linens tend to weigh heavy, especially when wet, and take longer to dry.

Light cottons are best in hot climates. Avoid polyester as it creates sweat. Performance fabrics, which are designed especially for sport or activity, are also good for travelling, hiking, walking, and sightseeing.

Merino or cashmere is thinner, lighter, and warmer than other wools.

Natural silk is a good all-rounder, keeping you warm when it's cold and cool when it's hot.

Unless you're 100% sure of the comfortability of a new pair of shoes, don't take them. All footwear needs to fit properly as well as look good, otherwise it becomes dead weight to carry around.

On footwear: inner soles can be a great comfort. All sorts of moulded insoles are available off-the-peg, and lambswool insoles are invaluable in cold climates worn in boots or regular shoes or just for added comfort.

### Some trusty essentials

Carry a sarong or scarf (preferably cotton) in your hand luggage. It can be used as a picnic cloth, pillow, or headrest cover, an eye mask when the light is too bright, a towel, a sunhat, a bag, a window blind, and various pieces of clothing. It's also useful to have this (or a warmer version, such as a pashmina or large scarf) to hand when in cold air-conditioned restaurants or trains.

Earplugs or good ear/headphones are helpful when trying to rest in noisy surroundings.

A compass is invaluable.

Even if you use online maps, carry a paper map.

Torch.

Needle and cotton.

Safety pins.

A teaspoon. Or a spork (a spoon and fork combined in one utensil).

A few plasters (for cuts but also good for blisters, or preventing them).

Antibacterial hand gel for when you don't have access to hand washing.

Folding fan (for beach and hot climates).

Folding sunhat.

Flip-flops.

Notebook and pen or pencil.

## What are carbon offsets?

Carbon offsets represent reductions in greenhouse gases that compensate for emissions from elsewhere.

Carbon offset schemes invest in environmental projects in order to balance out an individual's or company's own carbon footprint. Projects are often based in developing countries and designed to reduce future emissions. This might involve rolling out clean energy technologies, purchasing and ripping up carbon credits from an emissions trading scheme, or soaking up $CO_2$ from the air through the planting of trees.

Some people and organizations offset their entire carbon footprint while others aim to neutralize the impact of a specific activity, such as taking a flight. To do this, the holidaymaker or business person visits an offset website, uses the online tools to calculate the emissions of their trip, and then pays the offset company to reduce emissions elsewhere in the world by the same amount, thus making the flight 'carbon neutral'.

*The Rough Guide to Green Living*

## Leave No Trace

When camping or glamping, on holiday or at festivals, there is a best practice and philosophy in the wilderness community called 'Leave No Trace'. The principles reinforce the idea that we should respect and care for our wild areas and do our part to preserve and protect them as we enjoy them. Many of those principles extend beyond backpacking and into the ethics of sustainable travel everywhere and the inherent responsibility of those of us who travel.

Created by the U.S.D.A. Forest Service in the 1960s, Leave No Trace was seen as increasingly necessary as public land use expanded and land managers witnessed the biophysical effects of this use.

By the mid-1980s, the Forest Service had a formal 'No-Trace' programme emphasizing wilderness ethics and sustainable travel and camping practices. The success of this programme led to the Forest Service, National Park Service, and Bureau of Land Management's authoring a pamphlet entitled 'Leave No Trace Land Ethics'.

In the early 1990s, the Forest Service worked with the National Outdoor Leadership School (NOLS) to develop hands-on, science-based minimum-impact education training for non-motorized recreational activities.

## Leave No Trace principles

*Travel and camp on durable surfaces*

- Durable surfaces include established trails and campsites, rock, gravel, dry grasses or snow.

- Protect riparian areas by camping at least 61 metres (200 feet) from lakes and streams.

- Keep campsites small. Focus activity in areas where vegetation is absent.

*Leave what you find*

- Preserve the past: examine, but do not touch cultural or historic structures and artifacts.

- Leave rocks, plants, and other natural objects as you find them.

- Avoid introducing or transporting non-native species.

*Plan ahead and prepare*

- Know the regulations and special concerns for the area you'll visit.

- Prepare for extreme weather, hazards and emergencies.

*Respect wildlife*

- Observe wildlife from a distance. Do not follow or approach them.

- Never feed wildlife. It damages their health, alters natural behaviours, and exposes them to predators.

*Be considerate of other visitors*

- Be courteous. Yield to other users.

- Step to the downhill side of the trail when encountering pack stock.

- Let nature's sounds prevail. Avoid loud voices and noises.

*"A good traveller leaves no tracks.
Good speech lacks fault-finding."*

LAO TZU

*"A white explorer in Africa, anxious to press ahead with his journey, paid his porters for a series of forced marches. But they, almost in reach of their destination, set down their bundles and refused to budge. No amount of extra payment would convince them otherwise. They said they had to wait for their souls to catch up."*

BRUCE CHATWIN
*The Songlines*

*"Sometimes I think we're alone in the universe, and sometimes I think we're not. In either case the idea is quite staggering."*

ARTHUR C. CLARKE

## Slow travel

The more people live in the urban fast lane, the more they crave 'slow travel' as a counterbalance. To seek out a place to restore calm and serenity for a couple of weeks, to stay put in that one place, unplugged, to read, think, do nothing but spend time with a friend, a loved one, or alone is a refreshing tonic for mind and body.

Seekers of silence have to travel increasingly larger distances to find areas of real stillness, where light and sound pollution are absent, enabling enjoyment of the night sky and hearing only the sounds of nature.

Travel invariably involves a lot of waiting, especially at airports, train stations, and visa offices.

If delays or cancellations mean having to wait it out, the only option is to create a different attitude to waiting.

Find a place to sit and use the time to practise mindful breathing, catch up with your reading, or just let go and observe what's going on around you.

Once we're travelling we have to take the view that we are in the right place, wherever and whenever that is.

*"La vie n'est pas ailleurs."*
*[Life is not elsewhere.]*

JACQUES SALOMÉ

## Gap Year

Finding a job on a gap year can be a rewarding early work/life experience. Travelling and working away from home will give you an opportunity to understand a different culture as well as to develop confidence and independence.

In a world where international affiliations and contacts are held high, studying another country's history, language, and traditions is a valuable asset.

Improve your chances of getting ahead in a chosen career with work experience. Whether you want to work for a major blue chip company, a small business, or to develop your own entrepreneurship, shadowing someone already doing that role is a great way to gain the experience you need.

If you want to travel, you can still gain experience, either in a voluntary role or in a role that will pay.

Taking a year out doesn't have to be limited to after-school. Many people choose to take a career break to travel at different stages in their lives. This could be for numerous reasons – they may have been made redundant, had some life-changing experience, be looking for a new direction, or reached later life and want to experience a completely different lifestyle for a spell. Whatever the reason, most gap year organizations also cater for older people looking for a year's career break, and will offer work placements or gap year programmes whatever your age. Or you can have fun designing your own.

Undoubtedly there are positive contributions made by all types of 'volun-tourists', but it is not a foregone conclusion. There should always be awareness that the developing world is not simply a destination for relentless backpacking on a year off. A mindful traveller will consider all the implications of sustainability, question their real contribution, thoroughly research the countries and communities they plan to visit, and make decisions based on a combination of altruism, practicalities, and responsibility before embarking on a global spree.

Although you might be going away for as long as a year, it does not mean you have to take a year's worth of supplies. You will discard, replace, borrow, and buy along the way and, most importantly, use the same basics over and over again. Take the challenge: make travelling light a way of life.

*"I was heavily involved on all fronts: with mountaineering outfitters, who oddly enough never fathomed the depths of my ignorance; possibly because they couldn't conceive of anyone acquiring such a collection of equipment without knowing how to use it."*

ERIC NEWBY
*A Short Walk in the Hindu Kush*

## World Heritage Sites

The aim of the The United Nations Educational, Scientific and Cultural Organization (UNESCO) is to seek and encourage the identification, protection, and preservation of cultural and natural heritage considered to be of outstanding value to humanity around the world. This is embodied in an international treaty called the Convention Concerning the Protection of the World Cultural and Natural Heritage, adopted by UNESCO in 1972.

'Heritage is our legacy from the past, what we live with today, and what we pass on to future generations.'

**Paradox:** In poorer countries which host heritage sites there is often insufficient local governance in place to cope with sustainable tourism.

An example: Angkor Wat, a temple complex in Cambodia, and the Inca fortress of Machu Picchu in Peru are often cited as places of world-historical importance, but an influx of tourists may cause serious damage.

Mindful travellers can make their own contribution towards safeguarding sites by travelling out of season, avoiding large guided tours, not disturbing local infrastructure, and checking on the provenance of locally made artefacts.

Whenever an incident occurs that highlights the vulnerability of a tourist destination – earthquake, terrorism, or other disaster – the inclination of many is to avoid the place. But statistics show you are just as safe visiting the affected area as you are anywhere. The chances of an incident affecting our safety are no more than any journey we regularly make on the road. In fact the country or place that has been affected by such a disaster needs the revenue, so it is important to maintain a balanced view of where and why we travel, and how we spend our travel budget. If in doubt contact the relevant embassy offices for guidelines.

### Be mindful crossing the road

Wherever your travels take you –
take care whether you're in an
unfamiliar city or just going to
your local corner shop.

This is particularly pertinent when
travelling abroad and unused to the
direction of traffic. Some countries,
for example, allow cyclists to come up
one-way streets – often causing injury
to unsuspecting pedestrians.

Even as a pedestrian find out the rules
of the road.

Be aware, be mindful of the importance
of what you're doing – and where.

## Wherever you go, there you are

If you practise meditation or
mindfulness you develop a keener
sense of the place you are in, at every
moment. And wherever that place is, is
the place you're meant to be. Because
that is where you are.

*"The major occupation of Western civilisation seems to be to go some place else... Travel should be adding to people's life experience but I wonder if they aren't simply fleeing from experience. Some of them are literally in flight from consideration of anything that means anything. Especially for wealthy people, every moment has to be occupied with not being where they are."*

ARTHUR MILLER
*The Times, 4 July 2000*

## Quests

Journeys towards an actual or moral goal appear in the history and folklore of every nation. Such quests require great courage on the part of the hero or heroine in overcoming many obstacles to ultimately reach their objective.

What is – or what would be – your personal quest?

*"Ambition leads me not only farther than any other man has been before me, but as far as I think it possible for man to go."*

CAPTAIN JAMES COOK
*The Journals*

Travel technology has resulted in the separation of travellers from their surroundings. Hermetically sealed jet planes move travellers across the world on journeys that take a fraction of the time the same journey would be by land or sea. Convenience, urgency, and necessity make this an advantage, but it also separates us from our natural rhythms and does not allow for gradual acclimatization as the journey progresses. Our circadian clocks are thrown out of kilter, we have no sense of changes in culture, people, language, and climate so that we arrive out of sync with the natural progression of moving from one place to another.

"*No changing of place at a hundred miles an hour will make us one whit stronger or happier or wiser. There was always more in the world than man could see, walked they ever so slowly; they will see it no better for going fast. The really precious things are thought and sight, not pace. It does a bullet no good to go fast; and a man, if he be truly a man, no harm to go slow; for his glory is not at all in going, but in being.*"

JOSH RUSKIN
*Modern Painters, Vol. III*

Happiness cannot exist whilst
expressing hatred or anger, jealousy
or recrimination.

Practise mindfulness to avoid negative
and harmful emotions. Practise
mindfulness to free yourself up,
free to be happy on all your travels.

*"We are all affecting the world every moment, whether we mean to or not. Our actions and states of mind matter, because we are so deeply interconnected with one another."*

RAM DASS

*"As we jog on, either laugh with me, or at me, or in short do anything, – only keep your temper."*

LAURENCE STERNE
*Tristram Shandy*

When packing to travel – don't forget the importance of travelling light mindfully as well as baggage-wise. Just pack the core values – love, compassion and kindness. Leave behind the heavy stuff that weighs you down – resentment, regret, cynicism and anger.

It is a good principle not to let the sun go down on an argument, so it is with departures. Be mindful of leaving on good terms so that no regrets emerge in the days to come.

Partings are also inevitable with people we meet along the way; but better to have had the kindness of strangers, the meeting of minds, and friendships, than not to have had the encounters at all.

Good friendship and love remain embedded in our souls.

*"We shall not cease from exploration
And the end of all our exploring
Will be to arrive where we started
And know the place for the first time."*

T.S. ELIOT
*Little Gidding V, Four Quartets*

# BIBLIOGRAPHY

**Books and Journals mentioned in** *The Little Book of Mindful Travel*

Adams, Douglas, *The Long Dark Tea-Time of the Soul (1989)*

Barnes, Julian, *Flaubert's Parrot (1984)*

Bryson, Bill, *Neither Here Nor There (1991)*

Chatwin, Bruce, *The Songlines (1986)*

Cook, Captain James, *The Journals (1999)*

Davidson, Robyn, *Tracks (1980)*

Durrell, Laurence, *Spirit of Place: Letters and Essays on Travel (1969)*

Eliot, George (Mary Ann Cross), *Middlemarch (1874)*

von Goethe, Johann Wolfgang, *Italian Journey (1816)*

Grahame, Kenneth, *The Wind in the Willows (1908)*

Hesse, Hermann, *Siddhartha (1922)*

Jerome, Jerome K, *Three Men in A Boat (1889)*

Kerouac, Jack, *On The Road (1957)*

Levi-Strauss, Claude, *Tristes Topiques (1955)*

MacFarlane, Robert, *The Old Ways: A Journey on Foot (2012)*

Newby, Eric, *A Short Walk in the Hindu Kush (1958)*

de Mello, Anthony, *Awareness (1997)*

Morris, Jan, *Contact! Brief encounters in a lifetime of travel. (2010)*

Pirsig, Robert M., *Zen and the Art of Motorcycle Maintenance (1999)*

Rowan, Tiddy, *The Little Book of Mindfulness (2013)*

Steinbeck, John, *Travels with Charley (1962)*

Stevenson, Robert Louis, *The Silverado Squatters (1883)*

Theroux, Paul, *Ghost Train to the Eastern Star* (2008)

Twain, Mark, *Tom Sawyer Abroad* (1894)

Yutang, Lin, *The Importance of Living* (1937)

## Websites

www.breakingmuscle.com (for isometric exercises)
www.newscientist.com
www.sustainabletourism.net
www.whytravel.org
www.mindfulnessjourneys.com
www.nrdc.org/globalwarming/offsets.asp
www.theguardian.com
www.leavenotrace.org
www.gapwork.com
www.whc.unesco.org
www.seat61.com
www.low-cost-airline-guide.com
www.numbeo.com
www.rome2rio.com
www.bookgreener.com
www.nsca.com
www.travel.thetrainline-europe.com/interrail/
www.plumvillage.com
www.howtospendit.ft.com/travel
www.mindapps.se

## QUOTES ARE TAKEN FROM:

**Anatole France** was a French poet, journalist, and successful novelist

**Anthony de Mello** was an Indian spirtual teacher, writer and psychotherapist.

**Antoine de Saint-Exupéry** was a French writer and pioneering aviator. He is best remembered for his sucessful novella *The Little Prince*.

**Arthur C. Clarke** was an influential figure in 20th century science ficton. He was well-known for the novel and movie *2001: A Space Odyssey*.

**Arthur Miller** was a playwright and a prominent figure in twentieth-century American theatre. His best known play is *Death of a Salesman*.

**Bill Bryson** is a bestselling travel author whose works include, *The Lost Continent*, *Neither Here Nor There* and *A Short History of Nearly Everything*.

**Bruce Chatwin** was an English writer whose best known works include *In Patagonia* and *The Songlines*.

**Captain James Cook** was a British explorer and navigator. He charted New Zealand and Australia's Great Barrier Reef.

**Claude Levi-Strauss** was an internationally recognized French anthropologist and ethnologist.

**Confucius** was an influential Chinese teacher, philosopher and political.

**Douglas Adams** was a British writer, dramatist and humorist, best-known for his work, *The Hitchhiker's Guide to the Galaxy*.

**Ernest Hemingway** was a Nobel Prize winning author and considered one of the great American 20th century novelists.

**George Eliot (Mary)** was a English novelist and one of the leading writers of the Victorian era.

**George Eric Newby** was a British travel author and author of the classic *A Short Walk in the Hindu Kush*.

**George Leigh Mallory** was an English mountaineer who took part in the first three expeditions to Mount Everest in the early 1920s.

**G.K. Chesterton** was an English writer, philosopher and lay theologian.

**Gustave Flaubert** was an influential French novelist if the realist period, known best for *Madame Bovary*.

**Henry David Thoreau** was a writer whose masterpiece was *Walden*.

**Hermann Hesse** was a German poet and novelist. He was awarded the Nobel Prize for Literature in 1946.

**Ivan Turgenev** was a Russian novelist best known for his novel *Fathers and Sons*.

**Jack Kerouac** was a American novelist best known for the novel *On the Road*.

**James A. Michener** was an American author of more than 40 books.

**Jan Morris** is a respected Welsh historian, author and travel writer.

**Jacques Salome** is a French psychologist and writer.

**Jerome K. Jerome** was a humorist and author of *Three Men in a Boat*.

**Johann Wolfgang von Goethe** was a German writer and statesman and is considered the greatest German literary figure.

**John A. Shedd** was an American author and professor.

**John Steinbeck** was an American writer who recieved the Novel Prize for literature in 1962.

**Jonathan Raban** is a British travel writer and novelist.

**Joris-Karl Huysmans** was a French novelist.

**Julian Barnes** is an English writer and Man Booker Prize winner for his novel *The Sense of an Ending*.

**Kenneth Grahame** was the author of *Wind and the Willows*.

**Lao Tzu** was a philosopher and author of *Tao Te Ching*.

**Laurence Sterne** was an Anglo-Irish novelist and an Anglican clergyman.

**Lawrence Durrell** was an expatriate British novelist, poet and writer of topographical books.

**Lin Yutang** was a Chinese writer, translator, linguist and inventor.

**Marcel Proust** was a French novelist best known for his monumental novel *Remeberance of Thing Past*.

**Mark Twain** was an American author and humourist. He was the author of *The Adventures of Tom Sawyer* and *Huckleberry Finn*.

**Paul Theroux** is an American travel writer and novelist best known for his work The Great Railway Bazaar.

**Pico Iyer** is an acclaimed travel writer.

**Ralph Waldo Emerson** was an American essayist and poet who led the Transcendentalist movement in the mid 19th century.

**Ram Dass** a well-known and highly regarded American spirtual teacher and author of the best-selling book *Be Here Now*.

**Robert Louis Stevenson** was a Scottish novelist well-known for his works *Treasure Island* and *Kidnapped*.

**Robert M. Pirsig** is an American author and philosopher, best known for his philosophical novel *Zen and the Art of Motorcycle Maintenance*.

**Robyn Davidson** is an Australian writer well-known for her book *Tracks*, about her 1,700-mile trek across the Australian outback.

**Rumi** was a 13th-century Persian poet, theologian and Sufi mystic.

**Samuel Johnson** was an essayist and literary historian who was a prominent figure in 18th century England.

**Seneca** was a Roman Stoic philosopher, statesman and dramatist. He was a tutor and later advisor to emperor Nero.

**Thich Nhat Hanh** is a Vietnamese Zen Buddist monk, author and peace activist.

**T.S. Eliot** was a British poet known widely for his work *The Waste Land*. He won the Nobel Prize for Literature in 1948.

## PAGE REFERENCES

**Page 6:** Pirsig, Robert M., *Zen and the Art of Motorcycle Maintenance: An Inquiry Into Values* (The Bodley, 1974)

**Page 19:** Jerome, Jerome K., *Three Men in a Boat* (J. J. Arrowsmith, 1889)

**Page 21:** Stevenson, Robert Louis., *The Silverado Squatters* (Chatto & Windus, 1883)

**Page 23:** Yutang, Lin,. *The Importance of Living* (Reynal & Hitchcock, Inc, 1937)

**Page 31:** Michener, James A., *Good Advice* (1982)

**Page 33:** Pirsig, Robert M., *Zen and the Art of Motorcycle Maintenance: An Inquiry Into Values* (The Bodley, 1974)

**Page 37:** Theroux, Paul, *Ghost Train to the Eastern Star* (Penguin, 2009)

**Page 40:** Twain, Mark, *Tom Sawyer Abroad* (American Publishing Company, 1876)

**Page 42:** Davidson, Robyn, *Tracks* (Jonathan Cape Ltd, 1980)

**Page 45:** Macfarlane, Robert., *The Old Ways: A Journey on Foot* (Hamish Hamilton, 2012)

**Page 51:** Shedd, John A., *Salt from my Attic* (Jonathan Cape Ltd, 1980)

**Page 61:** Eliot, George, *Middlemarch* (William Blackwood and Sons, 1874)

**Page 64:** Levi-Strauss, Claude, *Tristes Tropiques* (Jonathan Cape Ltd, 1973)

**Page 69:** Hesse, Hermann, *Siddhartha* (Peter Owen Ltd, 1954)

**Page 77:** Kerouac, Jack, *On The Road* (Viking Press, 1957)

**Page 79:** Morris, Jan, *'It's OK to Stay at Home'* (New York Times, August 1985)

**Page 81:** Goethe, Johann Wolfgang von, *Italian Journey* (Penguin Classics, 1970)

**Page 84:** Steinbeck, John, *Travels with Charley* (Curtis Publishing Co, 1962)

**Page 85:** Iyer, Pico, *Why We Travel* (27th April 2009)

**Page 88:** Le Guin, Ursula, *The Left Hand of Darkness* (Orbit, 1981)

**Page 90:** Anderson, Susan Heller, *P.S. I Love You: When Mum Wrote, She Always Saved the Best for Last* (Rutledge Hill Press, 1920)

**Page 93:** Johnson, Samuel, *Letter to Hester Thrale* (July 2, 1784)

**Page 94:** Stevenson, Robert Louis, *From a Railway Carriage* (September 1, 1993)

**Page 97:** Flaubert, Gustave, *Flaubert in Egypt: A Sensibility on Tour* (Penguin Classics, 1996)

**Page 99:** Bryson, Bill, *Neither Here nor There, Travels in Europe* (Black Swan, 1998)

**Page 100:** Huysmans, Joris-Karl, *Against Nature (À Rebours)* (Penguin Classic, 2003)

**Page 101:** Barnes, Julian, *Flaubert's Parrot* (Jonathan Cape Ltd, 1984)

**Page 104:** Durrell, Lawrence, *Spirit of Place: Letters and Essays on Travel* (Axios Press, 1969)

**Page 107:** Anderson, Susan Heller., *Getting the Show on the Road* (The New York Times, 29th March 1987)

**Page 109:** Grahame, Kenneth, *The Wind in the Willows* (Methuen Publishing, 1908)

**Page 121:** Adams, Douglas, *The Long Dark Tea-Time of the Soul* (William Heinemann Ltd, 1988)

**Page 123:** Twain, Mark, *Innocents Abroad* (1869)

**Page 136:** Mello, Anthony de, *Awareness* (Fount, 1997)

**Page 155:** Chatwin, Bruce, *The Songlines* (Viking, 1987)

**Page 165:** Newby, Eric, *A Short Walk in the Hindu Kush* (Secker & Warburg, 1958)

**Page 171:** Miller, Arthur (*The Times, 4th July 2000*)

**Page 173:** Cook, Captain James, *The Journals* (Penguin Classics 1999)

**Page 175:** Ruskin, Josh, *Modern Painters, Vol. III* (1834)

**Page 178:** Sterne, Laurence, *Tristram Shandy* (Wordswoth Editions Ltd, 1996)

**Page 181:** Eliot, T.S., *Little Gidding V, Four Quartets* (1942)

**Publishing Director**  Sarah Lavelle
**Editorial Assistant**  Harriet Butt
**Creative Director**  Helen Lewis
**Designer**  Emily Lapworth
**Production Director**  Vincent Smith
**Production Controller**  Emily Noto

First published in 2016 by
Quadrille Publishing Ltd
Pentagon House
52–54 Southwark Street
London SE1 1 UN
www.quadrille.co.uk

Quadrille is an imprint of Hardie Grant
www.hardiegrant.com.au

Text © 2016 Tiddy Rowan
Compilation, design and layout © 2016 Quadrille Publishing Ltd

Reprinted in 2016
10 9 8 7 6 5 4 3 2

British Library Cataloguing-in-Publication Data
A catalogue record for this book is available from the British Library.

ISBN: 978 184949 769 5

Printed in China